Writing Tip Wednesday: The Writing Career Handbook

Mellanie Szereto

Writing Tip Wednesday: The Writing Career Handbook
Copyright © 2014 Mellanie Szereto
Published by Amatoria Press
Cover art by Dragonfly Press Design

All rights reserved.
No part of this book may be reproduced in any form or by any electronic or mechanical means, including information storage and retrieval systems, without written permission from the author. To request permission to excerpt portions of this book, please contact the author at mellanieszereto@hotmail.com.

ISBN-13: 978-0-9911473-5-9
ISBN-10: 0991147359

Dedication

This book is dedicated to every author, whether new or multi-published. Being a writer is often a solitary life and so many of you offer endless support to other authors by sharing your knowledge, advice, and encouragement. Thank you!

My wonderful online friends, I appreciate your visits to my blog and comments on my weekly posts. You never fail to bring a new perspective to the table. Many wishes for a successful writing career!

Many of the topics in this book have come from the discussions with my Indiana Romance Writers of America chapter friends. A single question usually leads to a dozen answers as we help each other on the road to our writing dreams. You're the best!

Preface

My Writing Tip Wednesday blog series began as an online writing craft resource for fellow IRWA chapter members and has developed into a pay-it-forward project in multiple aspects of writing and publishing. Numerous writer friends shared their knowledge with me when I started my publishing journey and I enjoy passing on that favor to others.

Through the course of an author's career, educational needs change from help with punctuation rules and POV to guidance on contracts and conferences. Creating, growing, and maintaining a healthy writing career shouldn't have to be trial and error. It consists of much more than writing stories. Be prepared. Be educated. Make well-informed decisions. Make writing a career.

Table of Contents

Part 1: Creating a Career
- Terminology......8
- Reference Materials......16
- Finish the Book......19
- Critiques & Beta-Readers......21
- Using Track Changes......24
- Types of Publishing......26
- Researching Agents and Editors......28
- Pitching......31
- Pseudonyms......34
- Publishing Contracts Part 1......36
- Publishing Contracts Part 2......38
- Publishing Contracts Part 3......40
- Publishing Contracts Part 4......41

Part 2: Growing a Career
- Edits......45
- Author Branding......48
- Author Websites......50
- Social Media......52
- Marketing and Promotion......56
- Blogging......59
- Professional Behavior......61
- Recordkeeping......64
- Business & Taxes......67

Part 3: Maintaining a Career
- Writing Organizations......70
- Conferences......76
- Workshops & Online Classes......79
- Conventions......81
- Writers' Block......83
- Fear of Failure...and Success......85
- Goal Setting......88
- Balance......90
- Reviews......93
- Piracy......95
- Hybridization......97

Part 1:
Creating a Career

Terminology

Terminology is an important part of writing and publishing. Knowing these terms gives the author credibility in the writing and publishing worlds. Communication with editors and agents is easier and the knowledge builds confidence so the author is better equipped to handle questions from readers, other writers, and interviewers. Workshops, classes, and conferences are less stressful for a prepared author. Writers can also supplement their fiction-writing income by writing non-fiction articles for magazines, blogs, and informational sources.

The terms are divided into sections, based on topic.

<u>Writing Craft Terms</u>

Author intrusion – inserting research facts designed to "teach" the reader; inclusion of social, political, religious, and economic views when they aren't important to the story's plot; using dialogue/dialect that doesn't fit the character's education/upbringing/location

Backstory/information dump – history of the character or information that is "dumped" into the story all at once instead of vital bits of information being fed to the reader as needed

Beta Reader – a person who reads the manuscript and gives the author feedback before the publication process to catch plot and character inconsistencies, pacing issues, areas that need clarification, and grammar/punctuation problems, depending on knowledge

Blurb – short description of the book designed to hook the reader; usually 25-150 words; used for promo and back cover

Character arc – the process in which the main character(s) grow, evolve, and/or change over the course of the story

Characterization – how the character's life experience has influenced who she is, how she interacts with others, her mannerisms, etc.; personality traits

Foreshadowing – subtle hints at upcoming conflicts and actions

GMC – goals, motivation, and conflict

HEA – happily ever after

Head hopping – changing point of view without proper transitions or breaks

HFN – happy for now

Misplaced/dangling modifier – adjective phrase that modifies the wrong noun

MS – manuscript

Pacing – the movement of the plot from beginning to end

Pantser – writer who begins writing the book without having a thought-out plot

Active vs. passive sentence structure – sentence in which the subject is doing the action vs. sentence in which the action is being done to the subject by someone or something

Pitch/elevator pitch – very brief blurb designed to draw immediate interest from an editor or agent; a face-to-face or online opportunity to "sell" your book to an editor or agent, using a brief blurb

Plotter – writer who plots the story before writing the book

POV – point of view

POV glitch – when the POV character shows things that can only be known by the other character(s)

Query – submission letter to an editor or agent

Synopsis – tells the chronological order of your story, using your characters' goals, motivations, and conflicts to describe what each character wants, why he reacts the way he reacts, and how those decisions and behaviors affect him and his growth (character arc) through the events that happen; also tells the progression of the plot and its resolution—whether it's permanent or temporary—and is written in present tense from a narrator's perspective

Tagline – brief phrase meant to spark interest in the book

Voice – intangible quality that adds depth and personality to a story; sets the mood and tone; influenced by word choice, punctuation, word order, and sentence structure

WIP – work in progress

World Building – process of creating the world in which the story takes place

Publishing Terms

Advance – money paid to the author in anticipation of royalty earnings. The amount is subtracted from any royalties earned. Generally, the author does not have to return the advance, even if it exceeds total royalties earned.

ARC – advance readers copy

Copy edits – checks for grammar, spelling, and punctuation; also verifies legal and usage questions and checks or questions facts

Developmental edits – edits for plot and character development

Digital-first publisher – publishes e-book version first and may also offer a print version at a later date

DMCA takedown notice – Digital Millennium Copyright Act takedown notice; notices sent by authors and publishers to pirate sites for the removal of pirated files

DRM – digital rights management: technology that limits the use of digital media for users

E-publisher – digital publisher; some also publish POD versions

ISBN – international standard book number

KDP – Kindle Direct Publishing

KDP Select – Kindle Direct Publishing exclusive

Line edits – checks the pacing, story continuity, and content

Nook Press – Barnes & Noble self-publishing venue

POD – print on demand

PW – Publishers Weekly

Royalties – percentage of the sale price earned by the author on sold copies

RT – Romantic Times

Self-publishing – publishing in which the author is the publisher and is responsible for all aspects of book production, distribution, and marketing, including but not limited to editing, cover art, and formatting expenses. The author receives all royalties directly from the chosen distributors.

Series or "category" romances – books issued under a common imprint/series name that are usually numbered sequentially and released at regular intervals, usually monthly, with the same number of releases each time. These books are most commonly published by Harlequin and Entangled.

Single-title romances – longer romances released individually and not as part of a numbered series. Single-title romances may be released in hard cover, trade paperback, or mass-market paperback sizes.

Subsidy/Vanity publishing – the production of books in which the author participates in the costs of production or distribution in any manner, including assessment of fees or other costs for editing and/or distribution. This includes publishing programs that withhold or seek full or partial payment or reimbursement of publication or distribution costs before paying royalties, including payment of paper, printing, binding, production, sales or marketing costs; publishing programs whose authors exclusively promote and/or sell their own books; and publishers whose business model and methods of publishing are primarily directed toward sales to the author, his/her relatives and associates.

Traditional publisher – print publisher; some also publish e-book versions

Genre Definitions

Contemporary Romance – Romance manuscripts that focus primarily on the romantic relationship and have a contemporary setting.

Erotic Romance – Romance manuscripts in which the sexual relationship plays an integral part of the plot, sexual language is explicit, and sex scenes are graphic.

Historical Romance – Romance manuscripts set in any historical time period.

Inspirational Romance – Romance manuscripts in which religious or spiritual beliefs (in the context of any religious or spiritual belief system) are a major part of the romantic relationship.

Paranormal Romance – Romance manuscripts in which the future, a fantasy world, or paranormal elements are an integral part of the plot.

Romantic Suspense – Romance manuscripts in which suspense, mystery, or thriller elements constitute an integral part of the plot.

Young Adult Romance – Romance manuscripts geared toward young adult readers.

Erotic Romance Terms

BDSM – bondage, discipline/domination, submission/sadism, masochism

DP – double penetration

D/s – Dom or Domme/submissive

GLBT(Q) – gay, lesbian, bisexual, transgender, (questioning)

TP – triple penetration

<u>Sexual partnering</u>

MF – male/female

MM – male/male

FF – female/female

MFM – male/female/male (men are not sexually involved with each other)

MMF – male/male/female (men are sexually involved with each other as well as the woman)

FMF – female/male/female (women are not sexually involved with each other)

FFM – female/female/male (women are sexually involved with each other as well as the man)

MMM – male/male/male (all men are sexually involved with each other)

FFF – female/female/female (all women are sexually involved with each other)

MMMF – male/male/male/female (men are sexually involved with each other as well as the woman)

MFMM – male/female/male/male (men are not sexually involved with each other)

Knowledge is power. It builds confidence and helps improve

writing by creating a strong foundation for a successful career.

Reference Materials

An author's library should consist of not only books in her genre, but Reference Materials to help with creating stories and preparing them for submission and/or publication. The following list contains my go-to craft and research books, but is by no means a complete listing of available resources.

Writing Craft:

Chicago Manual of Style
Published by The University of Chicago Press
ISBN: 978-0-226-10420-1
The most widely used style sheet/guide/handbook. It covers grammar, punctuation, and other important aspects of writing craft.

Writers Inc
Published by Great Source Education Group, Inc. (a Houghton Mifflin Company)
ISBN: 0-669-47164-X
An easy-to-use basic guide to grammar and punctuation for students. It covers grammar, punctuation, parts of speech, and writing process.

Plain English Handbook
Published by Litton Educational Publishing, Inc.
ISBN: 0-800-91793-6
An easy to use guide to grammar and punctuation for students. It covers grammar, punctuation, parts of speech, and composition.

Merriam-Webster Collegiate Dictionary
Published by Merriam-Webster, Inc.
ISBN: 978-0-965-43710-3
One of the most commonly used dictionaries in the publishing industry.

New Oxford American Dictionary

Published by Oxford University Press
ISBN: 978-0-195-39288-3
One of the most commonly used dictionaries in the publishing industry.

GMC: Goal, Motivation, and Conflict by Debra Dixon
Published by Gryphon Books for Writers
ISBN: 978-0-965-43710-3
A step-by-step guide to creating a strong foundation for fiction writing. It covers using goals, motivation, and conflict for strengthening characterization, character arcs, and plot.

And, of course...
Writing Tip Wednesday: A Writing Craft Handbook by Mellanie Szereto
Published by Amatoria Press
ISBN: 978-0-991-14732-8
A handbook of writing craft topics, including punctuation, grammar, writing technique, and preparing for publication.

Research:

English Through the Ages by William Brohaugh
Published by Writer's Digest Books
ISBN: 0-89879-655-5
A guide to word origins and dates of use. This excellent resource for historical writing covers word use from the mid-12th century to the late-20th century.

Mythology by Edith Hamilton
Published by Grand Central Publishing
ISBN: 0-446-60725-8
The classic guide to Greek and Roman gods. The Quest for the Golden Fleece, The Adventures of Odysseus, and many other mythology stories are included.

The Mammoth Book of Pirates by Jon E. Lewis
Published by Carroll & Graf Publishers
ISBN: 978-0-786-71729-3
Contains over 25 true tales of infamous pirates.

String Theory for Dummies by Andrew Zimmerman Jones
Published by Wiley Publishing, Inc.
ISBN: 978-0-470-46724-4
A beginner's guide to string theory.

Indian Mounds of the Middle Ohio Valley by Susan L. Woodward and Jerry N. McDonald
Published by The McDonald & Woodward Publishing Company
ISBN: 0-939-92372-6
A guide to mounds and earthworks of the Adena, Hopewell, and Fort Ancient peoples.

Medieval Arms and Armor: A Pictorial Archive by J. H. Hefner-Alteneck
Published by Dover Publications
ISBN: 0-486-43740-X
A pictorial guide to arms and armor from the 8th century AD to 17th century AD.

The Knights Templar by Frank Sanello
Published by Taylor Trade Publishing
ISBN: 0-878-33302-9
A history of the rise, reign, and fall of the Knights Templar.

Quite an eclectic collection, isn't it?

As with any research, verify the information with at least two reliable sources. Build a library, build knowledge, build a career.

Finish the Book

Writing is only one part of being an author.

Depending on the publishing path(s) you choose, the other demands on your time will vary—besides family, day jobs, etc. We all have to self-promote and communicate with readers through social media. Edits are a vital component of preparing a manuscript for publication. Conferences, conventions, and book signings can also be a part of a writing career. Keeping track of income and expenses is a must, whether you prepare your own tax returns or hire a tax specialist. A website requires maintenance and blogging takes time away from writing. What about building a brand?

While all of these topics are important, the number one priority of every writer should be to finish the (next) book. Without a complete manuscript, your chances of getting published are zero. Without the next book, your readers will find something else to read.

However, don't sacrifice your story to get it out to readers more quickly. Quality trumps quantity every time. Write a good story—and then write another one. We all write at different speeds and have different methods, so try not to compare yourself to others. Do what works for you and avoid measuring your success based on someone else's ruler.

Some suggestions for getting that book done:

1) Set daily writing goals.

2) Participate in #1K1H sprints with other writers.

3) Discover your best time of day to write and set aside a portion of it for writing.

4) Take a writer's retreat.

5) Brainstorm with other writers or friends.

6) Designate a reward for each chapter you finish or a larger one for finishing the book.

What motivates you to sit in that chair and write?

Critiques and Beta-Readers

Being part of a critique partnership or group is a personal choice. Some writers prefer to use beta readers or a combination of betas and critters. Others may rely on self-editing before submitting. Perhaps you need feedback faster than most critters can provide. As with most of the writing process, do what works best for you.

The first rule of critiquing is to point out positive aspects in the manuscript as well as problem areas. Use explanations and suggestions to help the writer make corrections. Critiquing is about giving and receiving feedback, not criticism. Keep in mind that a critique is one person's opinion and you don't have to follow every suggestion.

Don't expect your critique partner to catch every mistake. Even the best editors can miss simple errors. A less-experienced writer may not spot POV glitches, passive voice, or telling instead of showing, but the vast majority of writers are avid readers and will notice plot issues and character problems. You can't become experienced without experience. Critique partners and groups should complement each other, with each participant bringing strengths that offset another's weaknesses. You're building what should be a long-term relationship.

Be honest. I can't stress this enough. You aren't doing your critique partner any favors by letting major problems slide. Some things can be attributed to voice or the tone of the story, but writing craft weaknesses can't be improved if the writer is unaware. If you're wary of pointing out issues in the manuscript, this could be an indication you and your crit partner might not be a good fit. Use the first rule of critiquing for guidance.

Critique feedback can help you develop the thick skin you'll need to succeed in the publishing world. Not every person will like your story. Whether you agree or disagree with the feedback, make a concerted effort to let the comments and suggestions you don't like roll off your back. In most cases, your partner is trying to help you improve the story. If you suspect snark and non-constructive feedback, consider finding a new critter group.

Some partners/groups exchange crits online. Others meet in person. Some use a combination. Something to remember—we often misread meaning without face-to-face contact to read body language and hear intonation/inflection. Brainstorming usually works better with the immediate vocal response rather than thoughts put into written word.

We all have lots of responsibilities. However, repeatedly promising to return a chapter or manuscript by a deadline and missing it is a no-no. If you tend to be slower or know you have a particularly busy schedule, be up front about the amount of time you'll need to complete the critique. By the same token, be aware that your chapter/manuscript may not be your crit partner's first priority. Expecting to get your piece back the same day is inconsiderate—unless you've agreed about the response time prior to sending.

Critiquing is a great opportunity to get valuable feedback and learn more about writing craft, but finding someone you're comfortable working with is vital.

A few words on beta-readers…
A beta-reader reads through the entire manuscript looking for logic lapses, continuity and pacing issues, typos, and other obvious errors. Many times, this person is a reader rather than a writer.

Some suggestions for working with beta-readers:

Even if you know and trust your beta-reader implicitly, consider entering into a basic contract. This may seem like overkill, but, while uncommon, authors have been plagiarized by their beta-readers. Piracy can also be an issue, so protect yourself.

Set a reasonable time frame for feedback, like you would with a critique partner.

As with a critique, suggestions from a beta-reader are one person's opinion. The ultimate decision belongs to the author.

Your beta-reader should be an avid reader of the genre you're writing.

What works best for you? Why do you prefer that method?

Using Track Changes

Using Track Changes is standard practice for almost every publisher when editing manuscripts. Many agents prefer this method of noting comments, corrections, and suggestions in manuscripts. Some contests use it for feedback on entries. Every writer needs to know how to use track changes within a Word document.

Most times, Word will open with track changes already on if the document has been edited or critiqued with that method. If it doesn't, you can turn it on manually by going to the "Review" tab and clicking on the switch above "Track Changes" in Word for Mac 2011. You'll find track changes in a similar location in other versions of Word. Comment bubbles will appear in the right margin to show comments and changes. Look within the document for additions of commas, apostrophes, etc. You'll see a black vertical line in the margin wherever these additions have been made.

For anonymity as a contest judge, change the "Security" setting under the "Word" toolbar tab and "Preferences." Set "Security" to remove personal information upon saving the document. Some versions of Word allow the user to create a name to use for track changes, such as Judge 101 or Red-Pen Editor.

To respond to a comment within the existing comment bubble, click inside the bubble and type.

To accept changes and corrections made to the document, click on the checkmark at the top of the comment bubble. To reject and omit the changes and corrections, click on the X. The comment bubble will disappear when accepted or rejected, so do this only if you wish to delete the comment. Be sure to "Save" the document to save your changes.

To add a new comment, click on "New" under "Comments" within the "Review" tab in Word for Mac 2011 or similar command in other versions. A comment bubble will appear in the right margin near the location of the highlighted word you wish to address in the document. Sections of text may be highlighted if the comment refers to a phrase, sentence, paragraph, or scene. Type your comment in the bubble. Be sure to "Save" the document to save your comments.

Make corrections within the document while track changes is on to show where corrections have been made. A bubble will appear when spaces, letters, numbers, punctuation, and symbols are deleted from the text. The addition of spaces, letters, numbers, punctuation, and symbols will show in the default color or the color you've chosen for your comments. You can set your color choices by clicking on "Preferences" in the "Show Markup" drop-down menu. A vertical black line will also appear in the margin to designate the area. Again, "Save" the document to save your changes.

Now you know how to use track changes. Practice with critique partners, beta-readers, or during self-editing to get comfortable with it.

A word of caution about track changes...

When using the feedback of critiques, beta-reads, judged contest entries, and self-edits, ALWAYS make your changes in a clean document. Don't depend on those accept, reject, and delete comment buttons to make track changes bubbles disappear forever. Once in a while, they reappear when track changes is turned on. I've judged contest entries with comments in the manuscript before I've started my critiques. Don't let this happen when you're submitting to your dream agent or editor!

Track changes—Do you love it or hate it?

Types of Publishing

The publishing world is evolving faster than publishers, agents, and writers can keep up. Authors have more choices than ever before in regards to getting their stories into the hands of readers. Let's take a look at different Types of Publishing.

Traditional Publishers—This option is usually defined as print publishers like the Big 5 (or whatever it happens to be today) and Harlequin for romance. Most pay advances of varying amounts. Print (mass market paperback) is the primary format, but e-books are available for some imprints. Some of these publishers require agented submissions. Time from submission to release is often 1-2 years. Some traditional publishers also have e-release only imprints. The publisher is responsible for production and distribution costs.

Small Press/E-Publishers—This option is typically digital-first or digital-only release. Advances are unusual. E-books are the primary format, with print-on-demand books (trade paperback) sometimes made available, depending on sales, book length, or contract stipulations. Most of these publishers do not require agented submissions. Time from submission to release is usually significantly less than traditional publishers, often ranging from 2-3 months to 1 year. The publisher is responsible for production and distribution costs. Royalty rates are usually higher than traditional publishing royalties.

Self-Publishing—This option includes digital and/or print release at the author's discretion. Advances are not given. E-books are the primary format, but print-on-demand (trade paperback) is also available. Submissions aren't required. Release time depends on the author's schedule. The author is responsible for all costs associated with production, distribution, and promotion. Tasks like editing, book cover design, and formatting can be contracted out for fees. All royalties are paid directly to the author from the distributors at higher than traditional, small press, and vanity rates.

The author is the publisher.

Vanity Publishing—This option can include digital and/or print release. Advances are not given. The author pays fees to the vanity publisher for book production, distribution, and promotion. This business model does not follow the general rule that money should flow from the publisher to the author.

While I personally don't advocate choosing the vanity route, each author must decide which course works best for his/her needs. Weigh the pros and cons of each option. Take into consideration how you feel about the time frame to publication, royalty rates, upfront costs, and the learning curve associated with each path. Above all, do your research to make an educated decision!

Which way does your scale lean? Do you prefer more than one method (hybrid author)?

Researching Editors and Agents

In today's publishing world, Researching Editors and Agents has taken on new meaning. Not only do authors have more choices in their publishing paths, they also can choose multiple avenues, becoming a hybrid author. This leads to numerous questions.

1) Which publishing avenue are you pursuing (traditional print house, e-book/print house, e-book only house, self-publishing, or a combination)?

2) Are you researching acquiring editors, acquiring agents, or content/developmental, copy, and/or line editors?

3) Do you have a particular publishing house in mind for submission?

4) Does the path you want to follow require an agent for submissions?

5) If you've chosen to self-publish, do you want an agent for negotiating contracts for foreign/audible/print rights?

6) Do you write more than one genre? Will you need more than one agent?

7) Are you prepared to write synopses and query letters?

8) Will you participate in pitch sessions at conferences and online?

Once you decide on your avenue, you can see which questions apply to you.

If you're planning to submit to a publishing house that accepts unagented submissions, you'll need to research not only acquiring editors but their publishing houses as well. Be sure that house or editor publishes or edits the genre/subgenre you wish to submit.

Check their guidelines for details.

Follow publishers and editors on Twitter and like them on Facebook to see how they interact with authors and assess their general presence on social media. Get a feel for their personalities. Not every author will fit well with every publisher or editor. Take time to look at publishers' websites, their submission requirements, and editor profiles/bios.

Check "Editors and Preditors" and "Writer Beware" websites for information on bad practices and complaints. Ask authors who've worked with those houses and editors if their experiences were positive or negative. Were contracts problematic? Was the editing helpful, thorough, and professional?

If you're planning to submit to a publishing house that accepts only agented submissions, you'll need to research agents. Know what services you want the agent to perform before you query—representation as a submitting agent, contract negotiation for an offered contract, sales and negotiation of print, foreign, or audible rights. Think long-term needs.

Check out the agencies' websites, submission requirements, and agent profiles/bios. Agents have specific genres and subgenres they prefer. Don't waste your time and theirs by querying a genre they don't represent. Again, follow agents on Twitter and like them on Facebook to get a feel for their personalities. Some agents are more hands-on than others. Do you prefer more communication or less? Someone to take charge or someone to discuss every move with you?
Visit AgentQuery and QueryTracker for information on which agents represent which genres and whether they're accepting queries and new clients. Always go to the agent's website for the most up-to-date wish list, submission requirements, and instructions.

If you're planning to self-publish, you'll likely need

content/developmental, copy, and/or line editors. Content editors review plot and character development. Copy editors check grammar, spelling, and punctuation, verify legal and usage questions (like trademarked names), and check/verify facts. Line editors are usually responsible for pacing, story continuity, and content. Some tasks overlap, depending on the editor's skills. Shop Around!

Most reputable freelance editors have websites with a list of services provided and pricing. Contact fellow authors or join a self-publishing group for suggestions and recommendations. Ask for references and follow up by getting feedback from clients.

Finishing your book is only the first step in becoming a published author. Educate yourself on the industry and learn everything you can about publishers, editors, and agents before you take the next step. A bad publisher/editor/agent is worse than no publisher/editor/agent!

Pitching

One way to get your manuscript in front of an editor or agent is to pitch your book, either online or in person.

What is Pitching?

Imagine a 30-second to 15-minute job interview. In that short span of time, you have to spark enough interest to get a partial or a full request—the next round of interviews. A partial request can consist of anywhere from a few pages to several chapters from the beginning of your manuscript. A full request is the completed manuscript.

Yes, the completed manuscript. Unless you write very quickly and need very few edits, put off pitching your project until you've finished writing the book. A previously published author may, on occasion, pitch a proposal rather than a completed manuscript. The author has a track record the editor or agent can see, so the risk of making an offer with the book not being finished is much lower than with a new writer. A proposal is often the first three chapters and a synopsis.

If you have a copy of *Writing Tip Wednesday: The Writing Craft Handbook*, you might remember a section about blurbs and taglines. Use those short attention-getting, interest-sparking teasers as your pitch. They introduce the main characters, their goals, and their conflicts. Your pitch should make the editor or agent want to ask how your characters will overcome the conflict and achieve resolution. Be prepared to offer that explanation. Think synopsis here—ending included.

Editors and agents may host online pitch sessions on Twitter, a Facebook page, on a blog or website, or through some other social media. Use your editor/agent research to decide if the opportunity fits your genre. Read and follow the posted rules for the pitch sessions. Conduct yourself in a professional manner. That means thanking the host for his/her time and accepting your offer to submit or refusal for submission with grace. Do not behave rudely or belligerently to the editor, agent, or other pitching authors. The publishing world is small and close-knit. Behaving unprofessionally will earn you a reputation as such and discourage anyone from wanting to work with you.

Do not pitch on social media without an invitation to do so. Social media is for being social and promoting your books/blogs/etc., not for stalking editors and agents.

Conferences and conventions often hold editor/agent pitch sessions in conjunction with workshops and other events. These in-person interviews can be nerve-wracking and stressful. Start by dressing comfortably and appropriately. It's a job interview. Dress in business to business-casual attire. Be on time for your appointment. Remember that editors and agents are people too. They're looking for good stories and have more than likely been meeting with writers all day. Smile. Be friendly.

Don't feel like you have to memorize your pitch. Many times, a recitation of your blurb can sound wooden and simply memorized. Have a note card to help with the words if you think you need it, but know the basic premise of your story. Most of all, show the editor or agent that you love your story. Let him/her see your passion for writing.

Follow through when you receive a request. Send the requested materials in a timely manner and follow directions. If you receive and accept an offer elsewhere, let the editor or agent know that you're no longer looking for an agent or your manuscript is no longer available.

Last but not least, pitch only during appropriate times and in appropriate places. This doesn't include interrupting a private conversation in the restaurant, the bar, or the elevator. It also means the restroom is not the place to corner your dream editor or agent. Use good judgment.

Are you ready to pitch?

Pseudonyms

Your book is written, critiqued, and polished. You've begun researching your publishing options. You may have even started submitting and pitching.

Before that contract offer, you have to make another decision—to write under your real name or to choose one or more Pseudonyms. Some authors prefer a different pen name for each genre or subgenre they write. Others stick to a single pen name.

Writers choose to have pseudonyms for a variety of reasons. Perhaps your non-writing or your spouse's career would be adversely affected by using your real name. Maybe you want to protect your privacy. Do you write erotic and inspirational romance? Thrillers and children's picture books? Whatever your reasons, choose your pen name wisely.

Avoid choosing the name of a well-known author. Ignorance is not an excuse. Whether your intentions are above board or not, you risk people seeing you as trying to ride the coattails of another author. And, yes, some writers and publishers have used this method to get noticed and gain sales. Not only is it unethical, you may find yourself in a legal battle. At the very least, your peers will likely judge your choice tasteless and laughable.

Something else to keep in mind—pseudonyms and real names typically are not copyrighted. If you decide to use a common name, you'll find many other authors with the same or similar names. Should everybody sue? Of course not. Use your best judgment in picking a pen name. Conduct a reasonable search on Google or another search engine to see if someone in your genre is using the name. Chances are you'll find someone with the same first or last name or both. If a match appears for an unusual name (both first and last), I recommend going back to the drawing board.

Remember, you don't own your first or last name. Names are

simply part of language. If another author has the same or a similar name, she probably wasn't aware of your pen name. Unless you're a huge name in publishing, let it go. Rather than threatening legal recourse or bullying another author, recognize that your work will stand on its own. Use your brand to create uniqueness and interest. Spend your time writing instead of nursing your ego.

Above all, be professional.

Publishing Contracts Part 1

The day you've been waiting for has arrived. After months or years of writing, self-editing, and submitting, you finally receive an offer from a publisher. Are you ready to sign those Publishing Contracts?

In today's ever-expanding world of publishing, anyone can call himself a publisher. Did you research the company? Does the company have a reputation for treating authors well, having good editors, and paying on time? Are the contracts straightforward and fair?

Remember that when dealing with a publisher, money flows to the author. If the publisher charges for cover art, editing, promotion, etc., you're looking at a vanity publisher. While self-publishing requires an investment, the author doesn't share profits with any other parties.

If you haven't done your homework yet, do it BEFORE you sign the contract. Getting out of a bad contract isn't always possible, so learn what to look for or get a legal expert to review the terms prior to signing. Protect your interests and your rights!

Every contract needs to include your legal name, your pseudonym, title(s) of the book(s) being published under that contract, the publisher's name, and the date of the offer. The amount of any advance should also be stated, including how and when it will be paid.

What is the term of the contract? NEVER sign a contract without a defined number of years for publishing rights. Two to fifteen years are reasonable terms. Full term of the copyright is not. It currently means your lifetime plus seventy years in the US. If you discover you aren't happy with the publishing house, in many cases you're stuck after signing a contract with an undefined term.

In addition to term, the contract should state which publishing rights are included. Print, digital, audio, foreign rights—if the publisher doesn't offer some of these, why would you sign them away? Don't give up rights they don't offer!

Check for a section on royalties. What percentage is paid to the author for digital sales? This varies from publisher to publisher and averages 30-40% of gross sales from some retail distributors and net sales from others. How much is earned for print sales? Average print royalties are 6-8%. How often will the author be paid? Monthly or quarterly are most common, but also be aware that some publishers only pay when the author has reached a minimum payout amount for that statement period. If you were paid an advance, you won't receive royalties until you've earned out that prepayment.

Be sure to check the type of accounting used to determine payment of royalties. Basket accounting combines advances from more than one book/contract, and all advances must be earned out before royalties will be paid on any of the included books. This method is not in the author's best interest. Negotiate it out of the contract or don't sign!

Will your pen name be exclusive to the publisher? Some publishers offer special perks to authors who agree to exclusivity for a pseudonym. Be sure those advantages are listed in detail in the contract. With this stipulation, be prepared to create another persona if you self-publish or enter into a contract with a different publisher.

Are you writing a series that requires giving the publisher first right of refusal or exclusive rights to your characters or a unique species/world? If the publisher doesn't offer a contract for a book in the series within the contract-specified time frame, do you maintain the right to submit/sell to another publisher or self-publish the work? Some contracts contain a first right of refusal on any book or a specific number of books. All these issues must be addressed in the contract and should be negotiated.

Publishing Contracts Part 2

Are you ready for another look at Publishing Contracts? We barely scratched the surface with Part 1.

A lot of work goes into preparing a book for publication. All of these areas should be included in the contract. If you aren't able to negotiate acceptable terms, be prepared to walk away.

To protect both parties (author and publisher), the contract should contain an author's statement of original work. The author must own the rights to the work. This means no plagiarism, no works in the public domain, no other publisher can lay claim to rights, no copyright infringement, etc. Although some parts of the contract will seem like common sense, they have to be in writing to be enforceable.

The projected release date should be clearly stated in the contract. Does the release date apply to digital versions, print version, and/or audio version?

While many traditional publishers register the copyrights for the books they publish, many small presses do not. Self-published authors must decide on their own whether or not to complete this step. Is the author responsible for registering the copyright and its cost? Who is responsible for legal fees and filings if the copyright is infringed upon?

Will the publisher provide an ISBN for the book? They aren't mandatory for some retail outlets, but books without ISBNs aren't recognized by the big bestseller lists. How important is this aspect to you?

The publisher typically sets the selling price for all formats it provides. How is the price set? Are works with comparable length and subject matter used to determine the selling price? The contract should state the policy for discounting and special sales.

Does the author have the option of purchasing discounted copies?

The cover is probably the most important marketing tool for books. Does the author have input on the cover art? Can she ask for changes? The author should be provided with a cover art questionnaire to help the artist create an appropriate cover. Is the author allowed to provide her cover art at her own expense, subject to publisher approval?

Blurbs also attract buyers. Who will create the blurbs for your book? The author knows the story best, so most times she's required to write them. Does the publisher reserve the right to edit or rewrite the blurbs? If the publisher creates the blurbs, is the author allowed to provide feedback?

Another part of marketing is the title. Will the original title be kept? If it's changed, does the author have input or approval of the new title?

Editing is one of the most important aspects of publishing. How many rounds of edits will your manuscript undergo? The contract may or may not go into detail regarding editing, but you'll be better prepared if you discuss the procedure with the publisher prior to signing. Does the author maintain the right to accept or reject editorial suggestions? Remember, the story is yours. You should have at least some say in the final product. The contract should state that the publisher will notify the author prior to making any substantial changes. What happens if edits aren't returned on time? Is the release delayed or the contract terminated?

The manuscript also has to be formatted for publication. The publisher should be responsible for correctly formatting the book for all distribution outlets. If the publisher fails to complete this process and make the book available within a reasonable defined time period after the agreed upon release date, do publishing rights revert to the author?

How about we tackle promotion, marketing, and distribution in Part 3?

Publishing Contracts Part 3

We've covered a lot of territory concerning Publishing Contracts with Part 1 and Part 2 already, but we're not done yet! Now we'll look at promotion, marketing, and distribution.

In today's publishing world, the author is expected to participate in promoting her book. The contract should clearly state what promotional tools and opportunities the publisher will offer. The vast majority of us aren't going to get a publisher-paid book signing tour, but some publishers will provide books at no cost to the author for signings at major conventions and conferences. Will the publisher schedule a blog tour or place ads in RWR (RWA members' magazine), RT Magazine (Romantic Times), or other industry publications? What about online advertisements? How about reviews? Will the publisher send ARCs to reviewers or are you responsible for contacting reviewers and submitting your work?

Speaking of ARCs (advance reader copies), will the publisher give the author ARCs for giveaways and reviews? Yes, give—as in "free to the author." Print or digital format? Both? How many copies?

Part of marketing your book includes having a social media presence. Many publishers now require the author to have a website at the very least. What type of presence does the contract state? Website? Twitter? Facebook? Google+? Is the wording general or specific?

While marketing and promoting, you'll sometimes mention your publisher. Are you permitted to use the publisher's logo or other marketing tools? The contract should list which items may be used and in what manner.

Publisher websites often include author pages. Are you required to provide an author bio and photo to be included on the page and possibly in the book itself? Be sure to ask your photographer if you'll get digital rights to your photos. Many times they aren't included with the purchase of prints. Respect the photographer's copyright, as you hope others will respect the copyright of your book.

Distribution outlets should also be discussed in the contract. Almost all publishers sell their authors' books on their websites. In addition to that outlet, books may also be available from Amazon, Barnes & Noble, iBooks, Kobo, and several other online retailers. Which of these outlets will sell your book? Will your book be available at brick-and-mortar bookstores? While not all of these details are specifically outlined in the contract (because the publishing industry is changing too quickly to stay accurate), ask about current outlets to get a good feel for the breadth of distribution.

Publishing Contracts Part 4

In Part 4, we'll delve into the business-related legalese that puts most people to sleep. Be sure to check out Parts 1, 2, and 3 if you haven't already!

Hopefully, you've researched the publisher and found the company to be reputable and honest. However, bad things can happen to the best companies. Does your contract state the procedure for reversion of rights if the company is sold, becomes insolvent, declares bankruptcy, or shuts its doors? How will unpaid royalties be handled? Will the new owner be legally bound to honor your current contract? Contracts can be terminated under certain conditions. Are those conditions discussed and defined? What happens to any print copies of the book still in retailers' hands? If they aren't returned to the publisher, the author should receive royalties as usual until all are sold. If the books are returned, does the author have the opportunity to purchase them or will they be destroyed? The contract should address all of these potential issues.

On occasion, the publisher will initiate legal proceedings against an author or vice versa. What constitutes a breach of contract that may lead to this situation? In which state must the suit be filed, either by the publisher or the author? It should be the state in which the business operates.

Sometimes, changes in the publishing world can necessitate changes in the contract. Can the contract terms be changed by mutual agreement? What is the procedure for those changes? A good contract will also mention severability, meaning that if any part of the contract is deemed unenforceable, the rest of the contract remains in force.

Does the contract mention implied agreements? Nothing should be implied. Always have all agreements in writing before signing.

At the end of the term of the contract, does it automatically renew for a defined new term? Or does the author have to contact the publisher within a specific time frame to renew or request a reversion of rights?

The contract should have clear instructions on the author's right to request an audit of royalties and sales. The audit is most often done at the author's expense unless a minimum discrepancy is found. The contract should state that minimum percentage, along the time frame for completing the audit and how an underpayment/overpayment will be handled. Audits can usually be requested annually, or more often if the publisher has a history of underreporting. Be sure to compare royalty statement totals to the 1099-MISC form you receive for income tax purposes. Royalties paid during a given calendar year should equal the amount shown on the 1099-MISC.

Your contract may contain a confidentiality statement, restricting the parties with whom you may discuss or reveal details of the contract. Review it carefully, as it may be meant to keep all authors working with the publisher from comparing terms. If you're a new author, you may want to be able to get feedback from a lawyer, an agent, or a trusted friend with contract experience.

After you've signed, whether manually or electronically, be certain you receive a copy of the contract signed and dated by both parties. Contact information for both the publisher and the author should be included on the signature page.

A publishing contract is an agreement between the author and the publisher, where both parties should have fully defined rights and responsibilities. They have to work together, preferably in a positive atmosphere, with mutual trust and understanding.

Research publishers thoroughly. Read the fine print. Ignorance isn't an acceptable reason to invalidate a contract.

Part 2:
Growing a Career

Edits

Edits… Some authors love them. Some authors hate them. Either way, we all have to do edits—even those who self-publish.

Edits are usually grouped into three types, based on which aspects of the manuscript are being reviewed.
1) Content or Developmental Edits – checks plot and character development
2) Line Edits – checks the pacing, story continuity, and content
3) Copy Edits – checks for grammar, spelling, and punctuation; also verifies legal and usage questions and checks or questions facts

How many rounds of edits should you expect from a publisher? The number can vary, depending on that publisher's procedure. Sometimes a combination of content/developmental and line edits makes up the first round of edits, with copy edits being performed in the second round. Every manuscript should go through at least two separate rounds of edits. Like writers, editors often have strengths in one area or another, so having one round will likely mean missed errors or issues.

The timetable varies greatly from publisher to publisher. Traditional print edits tend to be spaced over a longer period of time than e-pub edits because the turnaround time from submission to publication is longer. Some e-publishers have first-round edits to the author within a few weeks of acceptance, setting a week or two later as the deadline for return. Final edits may be sent as late as a week to ten days before release, with a five- to seven-day deadline. Be aware that missing a deadline can push back the release date for the book or may even nullify the contract.

The turnaround time for a freelance editor depends on her client load and speed. Be sure to ask when researching content and copy editors for self-publishing. The waiting line may be months long for an experienced, in-demand editor. Costs can vary greatly too.

The big question…

Do I have to make all the changes my editor suggests?

The publisher wants to make your book the best possible product it can be so it sells well. The editor's job is to facilitate that process by correcting errors and suggesting ways to improve the story. However, the story belongs to the author, meaning she should have a say in changes. If a rewrite or expanded scene is requested, the editor should provide a reason for it. The editor should not rewrite or add to the book without notifying the author and receiving permission to do so. Always do a final read-through of the edited manuscript prior to publication. Unfortunately, editors have, on occasion, taken the liberty of making major changes without informing the author. While this may be grounds for breach of contract, the author is responsible for making sure her book isn't reworked by an editor without her knowledge as well as addressing that line-crossing with the publisher. Be proactive.

Simple mistakes, like missing punctuation or a misspelled word, are usually corrected with track changes turned on. The author goes through the manuscript, track changes bubble by track changes bubble, either accepting or rejecting the changes. Yes, the author can reject changes if she believes the editor's "correction" is, in fact, incorrect. Editors aren't perfect. An inexperienced one may not be thoroughly versed in the publisher's choice of house style and may make the occasional mistake. By improving her writing craft skills, the author is better prepared for edits and doesn't have to rely only on her editors for a well-written book.

Other issues have comment bubbles to show the author where clarification, expansion, or correction is needed. If the plot has a logic lapse, the editor should comment on the specific problem. She might make a suggestion on how to fix it or simply point out the issue. The author uses this guidance to clarify, expand, or correct the point within the manuscript. Track changes makes those additions and corrections visible to the editor upon return for verification.

Just as critiques should provide polite and encouraging feedback, edits should be helpful and positive. Snarky or unconstructive comments should be brought to the attention of the publisher. Be diplomatic rather than defensive. By the same token, edits are meant to improve the story and the author needs to learn to accept critical feedback. Taking edits as a personal attack shows the author isn't ready for honest opinions of her work. Unprofessional behavior on the part of editor or author can create an unhealthy relationship between the author, the editor, and the publisher.

The author ultimately has to decide which changes to make. If the publisher disagrees, be prepared to make some concessions or the contract may be terminated. Be open to suggestions, but remember the story is yours.

Author Branding

Every person, company, and organization in the business of selling a product or service must choose how she/it wants to be perceived by the public. This is called Branding. It plays an important role in website design, marketing and promotion, and social media.

You can use a tagline to help readers know what genre or sub-genre you write. Use broad taglines for multiple genres with the same/similar heat levels and more specific taglines for a single sub-genre. A sci-fi writer might use "Out of this world romance" to make her genre easily recognizable. "Romance you can sink your teeth into" could work for an author who writes only about vampires. For a more general impression, an erotic romance author who writes both contemporary and historical can try a tagline like "Sexy, sassy, sinful." Be creative! The tagline can be used on blogs, websites, and promotional swag as well as in signature lines for emails.

Themes can also help portray an author's brand. Dark, exotic colors and designs often imply paranormal branding, while flowers and pastel colors usually suggest contemporary romance or women's fiction. An author who writes stories set in the Rockies might use mountain-themed artwork for her website, blog header, or background. The theme can follow through to her Facebook cover and Twitter background.

Branding should be consistent on all social media outlets.

For marketing and promotion, use your tagline and theme to create items for giveaways and as part of book signing decorations and advertisements. An author whose books include crocheting might offer a gift basket with a copy of her book plus a couple skeins of yarn, a crochet hook, and the pattern for crocheted potholders for a raffle, drawing, or contest prize. Examples of her handiwork, some yarn, and several crochet hooks could be displayed on the table at a book signing. She can use crochet-related photographs or stock art in trade magazine and online advertisements with her book covers.

When your public persona has a brand, readers should be able to identify the genre of your books and find a common interest with you. Ideally, that common interest will attract those readers and encourage them to buy your books. As with covers, an author's brand has only a few seconds to capture and hold interest and turn a notice into a purchase.

Author Websites

An Author Website is one of the most important promotional tools a writer can have. It doesn't have to be expensive or fancy, but it should be up to date and easy to navigate.

Creating a website starts with choosing a domain name (the URL). Common names are usually already taken, so many authors add "Author" at the beginning or end of their names. Sometimes, the .com address isn't available. Using .net is an option, but consider how often readers may accidentally go to the wrong website. Is the other site for an author? A plumber? A porn star? Prices can also vary from hosting company to hosting company. Take time to do a little research before making this big decision.

The next step is deciding on hosting services. Some options like Blogger and WordPress offer free blog sites that can double as websites. Strictly website hosting services are also available and vary a lot in price. Some have upgrades for a higher fee, allowing the user to have more pages and access to more design options. Again, research is key to avoid overpaying for service.

Some website builders have templates and some require a fair amount of technical knowledge, including writing html code. Website designers offer many services to those who aren't adept at such skills for varying prices to build the site and additional monthly, semi-annual, or annual charges to maintain the site and update information when necessary. Compare costs and time.

Content is next on the list. Branding should be a large part of the artistic content. Stock art is a great option and can be purchased for relatively little money in many cases. All art should be used only with written permission from the owner if digital rights have not been purchased. Using licensed photos and illustrations without permission is illegal and can result in the owner not only requesting the work be removed, but pursuing legal action against the user. Artists don't like piracy any better than authors.

Be sure text portions are easy to read and free of errors. Use a large enough size and simple font for comfortable reading. Blurbs, excerpts, and informational text with mistakes can give the impression that the author's books will also contain misspelled words, misused words, and/or grammar issues. Authors can lose potential readers by not proofreading text on their websites!

The layout should be well organized and the color contrast should be eye-friendly. Too many intricate designs and harsh colors can distract. Some background/text color combinations are difficult to read. Simplicity usually works best. Take advantage of multiple-page websites by using a different page for each series, publisher, or genre. Works-in-progress, upcoming books, and contests for readers can fill the pages of a new author. Add book covers and buy links as well blurbs, excerpts, and future release dates. An organized site is easier to navigate. Consider a professional photograph with digital rights if including an author photo and biography.

Be sure to include links to all your social media platforms (Facebook, Twitter, Google +, LinkedIn, Goodreads, Pinterest, Amazon author page, blogs, etc.). Allow readers quick access to interaction. A single click is far more effective for connecting with readers and selling books than two clicks or a Google search.

Ask for feedback from friends, other authors, and readers. Use their comments and suggestions to refine the website and make it visitor friendly. When updates are needed, don't delay. Keep your storefront up to date for your readers!

Check out your favorite authors' websites. What features do you like? What can be improved? Do certain colors draw the eye? Which ones make reading difficult? A little research can provide insight into what works and doesn't work.

Social Media

Today's author is expected to do most, if not all, of her own promo and marketing. Social media plays a large part in making books visible, creating sales, and connecting with readers. Although many writers tend to be introverts and would much rather write than socialize, the days of publisher-paid book tours and advertising have faded into rarity.

So, what are the options?

Author Central (part of Amazon) offers author pages. Add photos, a bio, videos, and links to Twitter, websites, blogs, and events. Track Amazon rankings, check customer reviews, and look at sales information. Authors can claim all their books so readers/buyers can find all titles in a central location on Amazon. This social media site requires little attention, only updates as needed.

Goodreads allows authors to claim their author pages and books to create a place for readers to find out information about authors and their books as well as rate and review them. While Goodreads is designed for book ratings and reviews and not reader-author interaction, authors and readers can participate in book discussion groups. Authors can also run giveaways, enter book contests, advertise, and blog on the site. Like Author Central, Goodreads can be updated only when necessary, if preferred.

Another option is Shelfari (also part of Amazon). This site has virtual bookshelves for readers and is a self-described encyclopedia for book lovers. Authors and readers can post information about books and characters, series, family trees, etc. Shelfari also offers communities, book recommendations, and reader interaction. Again, day-to-day participation isn't necessary.

Statistics support the assertion by some that Facebook is the favorite place for readers to interact with authors. Facebook has profiles (designed for individuals) and pages (designed for public personas). Constant marketing and promo on profiles can land users in FB jail, as can posts containing nudity and other material that may be considered offensive to some users. A profile is great for staying in touch with family, friends, and even fellow authors, but buy links to books belong on a fan page. Pages allow for "likes" instead of friends and can be created for authors, their series, writing groups, reader groups, etc. Some pages permit author promotion of books, blogs, writing tips, and contests. Be sure to read the pages' rules for what can and can't be posted and how often. The same rule about posting artwork on websites also applies to Facebook. If it isn't in the public domain or hasn't been purchased, don't post it without the owner's written permission. Also, respect other Facebook users by not posting promo on their walls without an invitation to do so. This is called spamming and most people get very angry when it's done to them. Be prepared for un-friending, un-liking, and blocking if you choose to engage in the practice. The same can happen when authors send out mass invitations for others to "like" their pages, especially if the user has had no previous interaction with the person doing the inviting. This is also spam and is a practice everyone should avoid. Another increasing problem is new friends immediately asking people to "like" their pages via direct message or on the user's timeline. This behavior often leads to un-friending and blocking. Keep the "social" in social media.

Google+ is similar to Facebook but without most of the marketing rules and without the required friend confirmation. Connections can be added to "circles" designated by the user, like "friends," "family," "business friends," or "classmates." The user chooses whether the post is privately or publicly shared. Private posts can be made visible only to the "family," "business friends," or whatever circle is desired. Public posts are visible to all connections who have added the user to their circles and those who view the user's page. Posts can be "+1"ed, which is the equivalent of a Facebook "like," as well as shared. Like Facebook, Google+ has groups. These communities can be open to anyone or require approval to join. Invitations can be sent to join communities. Some allow promotion of books, blogs, etc. Follow the group's rules or risk being removed and blocked.

For authors who like to use visual aids as they write and want to share those with readers, Pinterest can be a good choice. This site allows users to "pin" photos, recipes, craft and building project ideas, etc. to boards. The photos may relate to period wardrobes, hero/heroine inspiration, or locations in a work-in-progress. Use photos in the public domain or with permission and avoid "pinning" those that may be considered pornographic or offensive material, as Pinterest has similar rules to Facebook regarding what content is allowed and what isn't.

Another social media outlet many writers use is Twitter. It's a fast-moving, 140-character way to post personal or promotional updates and interact with those with similar interests. Users can "follow" others and be "followed," without the requisite confirmation of Facebook "friending." While fewer readers seem to communicate with authors through Twitter, many industry professionals are very active and often offer writing, publishing, editing, and submission tips. Some editors and agents also host pitch opportunities and announce current wish lists. Although the vast majority of these publishing industry users are happy to answer writers' questions, they don't appreciate unsolicited pitches. Many users also will "unfollow" when spammed with direct messages asking followers to "check out my book," "check out my website," "check out my blog," "like my Facebook page," etc.

LinkedIn also allows authors to connect with other professionals. It's considered a networking site more than a social media outlet, but it can help writers find editors, agents, cover artists, marketing specialists, etc. The site allows users to ask and answer questions in addition to endorsing other users' skills.

YouTube can be used for book trailers, interviews, and advertisements. Some other social media outlets include Tumblr,

Reddit, and Triberr. The list could go on and on, leaving authors asking... Which are the best choices? And are they all necessary?

Rather than participating in everything and coming up short in all of them, choose those with the best mix for your time and personality. A few consistently good options are better than a dozen mediocre ones.
Remember—without the next book, they're all irrelevant anyway!

Marketing and Promotion

Although the majority of writers would prefer to spend all their time writing, part of being a successful author is actively participating in Marketing and Promotion. By using social media and the internet, authors can reach a large number of potential readers without a lot of expense. However, marketing and promotion require time and effort.

By posting regularly on Facebook, Twitter, Google+, etc., readers are already engaged when the next book gets its cover or is ready for release. They're more willing to share release day announcements and participate in contests, blog hops, and other events. By having a presence on a social media outlet, the author becomes more visible. Visibility helps sell books. As I mentioned in the Social Media section, etiquette is an important part of participation. Authors should post only on their own walls and in groups allowing promotion when having a cover reveal, celebrating a book release, or announcing a sale price.

Author websites and blogs are also primary places for posting release and pre-order announcements, new covers, contests, guest blog appearances, signings, etc. An up-to-date website or blog lets readers know the author is making an effort to keep them informed, and they're more likely to return that source for future information.

Book signings are a great way to attract new readers. Bookstores are usually the first venue that comes to mind, but they're far from the only possibility. Authorgraph offers readers online "autographs" for e-book purchases. Authors can sign up and add their books to Authorgraph's "library" of sign-able books.

Conferences are also a signing possibility. RWA hosts its annual Readers for Life book signing event at the national conference, with authors and publishers donating books to raise funds for local and national literacy programs. The American Library Association and the Public Library Association conferences are another possible opportunity for exposure through signings. Some writing organizations have booths at these conferences and allow members to donate and sign books during the event. Writing group and chapter conferences may also have book signings, with some permitting authors to sell books to attendees rather than donating them. While selling books earns money for the author, donated books are tax deductible, if provided at cost to the author (not free ARCs or publisher supplied), and can help with that difficult to achieve commodity "visibility."

Reader-author conventions typically have book signings, with readers purchasing the books on-site from either a bookseller or the author. The Romantic Times (RT) Convention and Lori Foster's Reader-Author Get Together are a couple examples of this type of convention. The event usually focuses on interaction between readers and authors more so than writer education and workshops like conferences. Be sure to bring plenty of cash to make change and think about using a credit card reader like Square to increase sales. A small fee (currently 2.75% for Square or 2.75 cents per dollar) is deducted from the author's sales for the service. It's very simple to set up and use.

Librarians and libraries are a great largely untapped resource. Developing relationships with them can provide opportunities for signings, meet-and-greets, and book discussion groups. A donation of the latest title may lead to sales if library patrons like the book.

Blog hops and blog parties can be free or paid. The author typically offers a prize to one or more participants—a signed print book, e-book, gift card, etc. Again, these donated prizes may be tax deductible and can increase visibility. Depending on her budget, an author might choose to purchase blog-hop services from a book promoter. Ask other authors for recommendations and research all promoters and marketers prior to signing a contract or making an oral/written agreement (phone or email).

Writer friends and colleagues who host guest authors on their blogs are another valuable resource. Reciprocate, if possible, and be sure to thank the host for providing an opportunity to showcase you and your latest release. Increase visibility by posting blog links to social media outlets. Don't expect the host to do all the promoting.

Authors can purchase advertising through book promotion/review blogs and websites, Facebook, Goodreads, Amazon, BookBub, The Fussy Librarian, and many others. This avenue also depends on the author's budget. Some are inexpensive. Some can be pricey. Research the options, costs, and typical returns on investments before forking over large sums of money to an unknown factor.

Newsletters can be an effective marketing tool, but they require preparation, regular releases, and time spent compiling a subscriber list. Services like MailChimp can assist with templates. Some online newsletter services are free and some charge a fee. Again, take time to research and ask for feedback from others who have used these services.

Marketing and promotion can became time consuming if an author tries to do everything. Try a few tools and weigh the effectiveness of each one. If one doesn't seem to work well, try a different one. Not every outlet will produce the same results for every author, and the best marketing tool of all is the next book.

Blogging

In addition to using guest blogs for promoting releases, authors can build a following by Blogging on their own sites. A themed blog helps boost an author's brand, expands social media exposure, and adds a different approach to marketing and promotion.

Some writers enjoy sharing their day-to-day experiences with readers or blogging about their writing processes. Others blog about themes they've incorporated into their stories, like knitting or gardening. Historical authors might choose to blog about clothing, food, and housing from a specific time period. Sci-fi writers may post articles on particle theory or space exploration. By taking advantage of this outlet, authors can potentially gain new readers and form discussion groups on topics related to their books.

When using pictures on blogs, be sure to purchase photographs and illustrations or post items from the public domain. As I've mentioned before, artists don't appreciate piracy of their work any more than authors. If caught using pirated work, bloggers may receive takedown requests and may be sued for illegal use of a copyrighted image. Be aware of the consequences.

Authors can also incorporate their non-fiction work into blogs. Numerous writers offer posts on writing and publishing. Some focus on grammar and writing craft. Others address the world of social media and advise writers on self-publishing. Whatever the topic, have firsthand knowledge or thoroughly research to provide accurate information. Misinforming blog readers/followers can have a negative effect on the author's reputation and sales.

Blogs are a great way to build relationships with fellow authors. Instead of focusing solely on marketing and promoting her own books, an author can help others gain exposure and create a supportive writer community. Host an author and possibly receive a reciprocal gesture in return.

Blogging isn't for everyone. It belongs in the pick-and-choose realm with Facebook, Twitter, Google+, and the rest of the social media options. Posting on a regular basis is vital to a successful blog. Choose to blog and do it well. Or choose alternate ways to expand visibility and do them well.

Professional Behavior

The topics of edits, author branding, websites, social media, marketing and promotion, and blogging all lead to one very important aspect of being an author—Professional Behavior. Any and all missteps can have significant consequences.

The worst possible indiscretion is plagiarism. Three words... DON'T DO IT. Copying an author's work does not make a person a writer. It makes her a thief. It's illegal and on the same level with piracy. In the age of the internet, plagiarism is very easy to detect and could land the accused in a lawsuit.

The next author-behaving-badly misdeed involves reviews. Authors should never, ever, ever rate or review a book poorly with the intent to increase her own sales or rankings. Yes, writers are readers and they have opinions about the books they read. However, trashing someone's book without reading it or with the sole purpose of making it less appealing to buyers will likely cause a backlash from the author's loyal readers and writer friends. If an author reads a book and is compelled to write an unfavorable review, she should include constructive comments and accurate examples of the book's problems. Think twice about leaving a less-than-glowing review under a pen name. Whether honest or not, the review reflects on the reviewer-author. If an author is on the receiving end of a poor review, her best course of action is to ignore it. Refrain from engaging or responding to the reviewer, even if the review makes mistakes about plot problems, character names, etc. Some people live for putting down others. Don't sink to that level.

Everyone has his/her own political, religious, economic, etc. views, but arguing about them on Facebook and Twitter—where editors, agents, readers, and fellow authors may see—probably isn't a wise choice. Don't bait others into commenting and don't succumb to baiting unless you're willing to deal with the fallout. Loss of readers, loss of book sales, etc. First impressions are difficult to change.

Although unauthorized use of images got several mentions in previous topic posts, it bears mentioning again. Purchase or use free images from reputable stock image sites or get permission from the photographer or artist for original artwork. Piracy is stealing, whether the commodity is books or art. Respect the artist and her right to make a living from her hard work.

Facebook etiquette can't be repeated enough. Do not friend people and immediately spam them with private messages or posts on their walls about your books, blogs, websites, publishing services. More often than not, that kind of behavior earns an "un-friending" and a block. Social media is social first and foremost. Marketing and promotion posts belong on the author's own timeline. "Be sure to like my author page to see all my updates!" with a link in a status post provides an opportunity for others to like the page if they wish to—without being spammed.

Return edits on time. Part of being a published author is behaving like a professional one and that includes prompt attention to time-sensitive responses, like edits, cover art questionnaires, and contracts.

Blog posts should refrain from insulting authors, readers, publishers, editors, agents, etc. Informational and educational articles can make others aware of unethical practices, but the advice must be based on actual evidence, not hearsay. He told her and she told me his second cousin twice removed heard that No-name Publishing is underpaying royalties could easily turn into slander. A warning can be issued without finger-pointing when carefully worded. Bad-mouthing others can result in retaliation.

An author can brand herself a diva by her treatment—or mistreatment—of fans or other authors. Without readers, an author has no audience. Treat them with respect and appreciation. Author A may have hit the New York Times Bestseller List, but that doesn't necessarily mean she's a better writer than Author B. It simply means she sold more books. A lot more than writing ability influences the publishing industry and sales. Keep the ego in check.

Today's publishing world is small. Word of an author's behavior can quickly spread between publishers, editors, agents, authors, and readers. Writing is a job/career like any other. Do your best to create and maintain a professional reputation.

Recordkeeping

Because writers often lean more toward creative thought, the mention of expenses, receipts, and mileage records makes many authors cringe. However, Recordkeeping is a necessary task. Not only does it aid in preparing tax returns, it helps writers budget for conferences, conventions, and other promotional opportunities.

Choosing a method is often the hardest decision. An envelope or a shoebox full of receipts to tally at year's end? An Excel spreadsheet with weekly or monthly entries and columns for every category of expense? A notebook with a listing of dates and their accompanying expenditures and mileage? And what about recording royalties?

Expenses…

The shoebox/envelope choice doesn't really lend itself to budgeting, but that's the method some authors prefer. To aid in tallying for tax time, consider writing a short explanation on each receipt (dinner meeting with editor; toll fees for RT trip; research books). Whether using self or professional preparation for tax returns, expenses should be categorized.

Spreadsheets and notebooks with timely entries both offer better opportunities to budget for future expenses. Expenses are recorded as they occur, leaving little chance of forgetting the reason for each receipt. Receipts can be scanned and stored in a recordkeeping folder in case the originals are misplaced or destroyed. Expense categories can be broad (Advertising & Promotion) or specific (Book signings; Blog Giveaways; Website Expense; BookBub Ads). Adjustments can be made to the recordkeeping system as needed by adding additional categories/columns. Meals should be totaled separately from other expenses since they have a different rate at which they're tax deductible. Auto expenses and mileage should also be recorded in their own categories for the same reason.

Detailed records can often mean the difference between a quick, uneventful audit and a long, painful one. Inadequate records may result in some expenses being disallowed, changing the end result of a tax return. Choose a method and start now!

Income...

Royalty statements record income from the sale of books. All publishers, including KDP, Nook Press, and other self-publishing platforms, should issue royalty statements with payments or make them available to download. How often—monthly, quarterly, biannually, annually—depends on the company and the contract. While the statements may contain a breakdown of which books sold how many copies, they may or may not list the sources of those sales. For example, one publisher's quarterly royalty statements might itemize the number of copies sold and royalty amounts for each retail outlet (the publisher website, Amazon, B&N, etc.). Other publishers may only list book titles and each title's total royalty amounts from all outlets. Some monthly statements list each country where the book is available for sale, the number sold and returned, royalty amounts, and conversion to the author's chosen currency. Information included on royalty statements is by no means universal.

Authors may elect to hand sell their books as well. These sales should also be recorded and reported, depending on the source of the books. The royalties from hand-sold books equals the amount the author paid for the book plus any shipping/handling fees minus the selling price. If the author purchased ten copies of her self-published print book from Createspace at $3.00 each and paid an additional $8.00 for shipping, her total cost would be $38.00. Her cost per book is $3.80. If she hand sells those copies for $5.00, her profit (royalty amount) is $1.20 per book or $12.00 for all ten books. Some publishers offer their authors discounted copies on which no royalties are paid. If the author hand sells the books at cover price, her royalties are figured the same as above—[(total book cost plus shipping) divided by number of books purchased] equals cost per book—and should be reported as such. When an author buys copies for resale from a retailer without an author discount, royalties have already been paid to the author on the book, so reselling under these circumstances doesn't require recording and reporting of additional royalties. Free ARCs from the publisher that are sold by the author should usually include the full sale price as royalties since royalties often haven't been paid on those books and the books were provided at no cost to the author. Books purchased by the author and given away are considered a promotional expense.

To aid in recordkeeping of hand sales, I created a receipt record to email to purchasers, in addition to recording hand sales on a spreadsheet. Many authors claim book purchases as business expenses, so this method allows for a printable or email-able receipt for buyers' tax returns—a must in case of an audit. For emailed receipts, Microsoft Word has several receipt templates that can be customized to meet the needs of authors hand-selling books. To provide a paper receipt, check with local office supply stores for two-part receipt books—one copy for the buyer and one copy for the seller. The purchase of receipts books is an expense!

Keep a record of all writing-related expenses and their paper or online receipts. Check with a tax professional when unsure if an expense is allowable. Keep a record of all sales, whether from royalty statements or hand sales. Whether an author completes her own tax return or hires a professional tax preparer, good records are a must.

Business & Taxes

Writing is a Business and writers have to pay Taxes, like any other business. The type of business depends on the author's preference. Several factors can influence which type of business will work best for each individual, including but not limited to amount of income and expenses and use of paid assistants or other employees.

In some cases, writers choose to be self-employed (sole proprietorship)—which means filing a schedule C at tax time and possibly paying quarterly self-employment taxes to avoid penalties for underpayment. Since an employer isn't contributing half the tax to social security and Medicare like a typical job, the self-employed taxpayer pays the full amount, based on net earnings (profits). All expenses and income are used to figure a profit or loss for the year. This amount is used to calculate the self-employment tax and is also included in the individual's tax return to help calculate the amount of income tax owed or refund due.

Rather than being a sole proprietorship business, some authors choose to become an LLC—limited liability company. Business and personal finances are separate to add protection from liability, meaning the owners of the company usually aren't liable for the company's debts. All states charge an annual fee to maintain an LLC business and many require an annual report or statement of information. Some also have state taxes. LegalZoom.com is a good resource for information on business types.

Another option for authors is incorporation, with either a C or S corporation. Like the LLC, business and personal finances are managed separately, and the owner(s) aren't usually liable for the company's debts. Articles of incorporation must be filed with the company's home state. Even if the corporation has only a single shareholder, it must hold an annual meeting and important corporate decisions should be recorded in meeting minutes. Some states may charge an annual filing fee for corporation status. A "C" corporation is taxed on net earnings and the shareholders are taxed on distributions, meaning the author is taxed twice if she's a shareholder in the corporation. Income of "S" corporations is taxed at the shareholder level only, making this type the better choice in most cases.

If the business has employees, including the author, an Employer Identification Number (EIN) is required and can be obtained from the IRS. Most states also require tax identification numbers issued by their revenue departments when a business sells goods and/or hires employees.

Since rules vary from state to state, options should be thoroughly researched. The IRS and each state's department of revenue website contains information on each business type and its filing requirements. A tax professional or business law expert can also help determine the most beneficial choice, based on the individual's needs. These links also provide easy-to-understand explanations about the business types and their advantages and disadvantages:
http://www.forbes.com/sites/robertwood/2012/05/03/c-or-s-corporation-choice-is-critical-for-small-business/
http://www.woodllp.com/Publications/Articles/pdf/Choice.pdf
http://www.woodllp.com/Publications/Articles/pdf/Tax_and_Liability.pdf

Remember to include consultation, setup, and filing fees in an itemized recordkeeping spreadsheet, along with all other writing-related expenses. Record mileage for writing-related trips, national and local dues for writing organization memberships, travel expenses for research/writing-related meetings/conferences/conventions, meals, office expenses, promotion/advertising expenses, contest entry fees, research/resource books, subscriptions, self-publishing expenses, etc. All expenses related to writing should be recorded for the business, whether the author chooses sole proprietorship, LLC, or incorporation.

Part 3:
Maintaining a Career

Writing Organizations

A great way to become an educated author is to join a professional Writing Organization (or two or three, if writing across multiple genres). While some limit membership to published or multi-published authors, some focus on educating new, unpublished writers as well as published ones. Many organizations offer discussion forums, workshops, conferences, critique groups, and other benefits.

The writers' groups in the list below are either national or international organizations. Several have regional, local, and/or online chapters, which may require an additional membership fee. The majority are genre specific, as fiction writing differs slightly from one genre to another. This is by no means a complete list. A Google search of "writing organizations" and the genre will yield more results. I've also included a regional writing organization that focuses on education, offering workshops and conferences for all writers. Please note that dues and membership requirements are subject to change. Refer to the organizations' websites for the most up-to-date information.

1) RWA (Romance Writers of America) – Members must be 18 years of age or older. Membership consists of three levels – General (for published and unpublished writers actively pursuing a career in the romance fiction genre) $95/year plus a $25 processing fee for new and reinstated members; Associate (for writers of other genres, those who write as a hobby, and acquiring editors, agents, and publishers) 95/year plus a $25 processing fee for new and reinstated members; Affiliate (for librarians and booksellers) $10/year plus a $25 processing fee for new and reinstated members. In addition to national membership, RWA has more than 145 international, local, and online chapters. RWA offers free and/or paid online workshops and a monthly magazine to members as well as its annual national conference to members and non-members. The organization also sponsors the Golden Heart and

RITA Awards for unpublished and published romance authors.
http://www.rwa.org

2) NINC (Novelists, Inc.) – International membership consists of a single level. NINC accepts multi-published authors only and has specific income requirements. Check the website for more information. Dues are $65/year plus a $15 application fee. The application process can take up to two months with the verification of publication and income information. Its focus is on the needs of career novelists in all fiction genres, and only members and industry professionals may attend the annual conference. NINC produces a monthly newsletter for its members.
http://www.ninc.com

3) SinC (Sisters in Crime) – SinC is an organization for the mystery genre. National membership consists of two levels of membership – Professional (published and unpublished authors pursuing a career in mystery writing and booksellers, publishers, librarians, editors, or one who has a business interest in promoting Sisters in Crime) $40/year, $80/2 years, $400/lifetime; Active (those who do not have a business interest in Sisters in Crime, including but not limited to fans and readers) $35/year, $70/2 years, $350/lifetime. In addition to national membership, SinC has nearly 50 chapters in the US and Canada. Members receive a quarterly newsletter and can participate in an organization-wide critique group.
http://www.sistersincrime.org

4) HWA (Horror Writers Association) – HWA is for published authors in dark literature. Active members are published professional writers of horror (required minimum number of publications, word counts, and income). Affiliate members must be minimally published (example: receive $25 or more for a 500-word story in the genre). Non-writing professionals (publishers, booksellers, librarians, agents, etc.) may join at the Associate level. Annual membership dues for Active, Affiliate, and Associate levels are $69/year. Supporting members are non-professionals

who would like to explore and share their interest in horror. Dues for this level are $48/year. HWA currently offers six regional chapters, a mentoring program, and networking through several events held each year.
http://www.horror.org

5) SFWA (Science Fiction and Fantasy Writers of America) – SFWA represents the science fiction, fantasy, and horror genres and has five levels of memberships. Active membership is based on a minimum number of paid sales for a minimum income to an eligible publisher. ($90/year dues) Associate membership also requires a paid sale to a qualifying market, but at a lesser scale than the Active membership. ($80/year dues) Affiliate membership is open to those with professional involvement in the science fiction or fantasy genres and are not eligible to become Active or Associate members. ($70/year dues) Institutional membership is for schools, universities, libraries, etc. and applicants must present credentials and provide references from three Active members. ($110/year dues) Those representing the estate of an Active member may apply for Estate membership. ($80/year dues) SFWA is also the creator and sponsor of Writer Beware, an excellent resource for those researching the publishing industry, publishers, agents, and contracts.
http://www.sfwa.org

6) MWA (Mystery Writers of America) – MWA focuses on crime fiction and non-fiction writing. The organization has four categories of membership, all of which cost $95/year for dues. Active membership is open to professional writers in the US who are published in the crime, mystery, or suspense genres by approved publishers. Associate membership is open to professionals in the US who work as publishers, editors, agents, booksellers, librarians, etc. Affiliate membership is open to crime/mystery/suspense writers who are not yet professionally published, unapproved publishers, unpaid reviewers, and fans. Corresponding members are those who qualify for any of the above classification, but live outside the US. MWA has regional

chapters for no additional cost to members.
http://www.mysterywriters.org

7) HNS (Historical Novel Society) – HNS promotes historical fiction and membership is open internationally to all readers and writers. Dues are $50/year. Published members receive free promotion of their historical fiction books. Reader members are encouraged to write reviews and most feature articles published by HNS on the website and in their magazine are written by members. The organization offers critique groups, conferences, and thirteen local chapters in the US and UK.
http://www.historicalnovelsociety.org

8) WWA (Western Writers of America) – WWA is open to published authors whose subject matter deals with the American West. Active membership is granted to multi-published authors in the genre. ($75/year dues) Associate membership requires publishing credits on a smaller scale and is also open to publishers, agents, booksellers, librarians, etc. ($75/year dues) Sustaining membership is granted to Active and Associate members who wish to further contribute to WWA. ($150/year dues) Patron membership is for companies, corporations, organizations, and individuals with a vested interest in the literature and heritage of the American West. ($250/year dues) WWA offers a national convention and regional, state, and local seminars.
http://www.westernwriters.org

9) SCBWI (Society of Children's Book Writers and Illustrators) – SCBWI is the only international professional organization for writers and illustrators of children's literature. Full membership is open to those whose books, poems, stories, illustrations, photos, etc. have been published or produced. ($95 dues for the first year and $80/year thereafter) Associate membership is open to unpublished authors and illustrators in children's literature and media. Journalists, bloggers, teachers, librarians, and those with an interest in children's literature may also join at the Associate level. ($95 dues for the first year and $80/year thereafter) SCBWI offers

networking, an annual conference, informational podcasts, an online bookstore for its published members, over 80 local and regional chapters, and a speakers' bureau.
http://www.scbwi.org

10) ACFW (American Christian Fiction Writers) – ACFW is an international organization for those in the Christian fiction genre. Membership is open to published and unpublished authors, editors, agents, and librarians. ($65 for first year dues and $45/year thereafter) ACFW offers writing courses, critique groups, an annual conference, and local and regional chapters.
http://www.acfw.com

11) Authors Guild – The Authors Guild is an advocate for published writers' interests. It provides legal assistance and web services to its members. General membership requires a minimum number of approved publications with a minimum income. Associate membership also requires publication, but includes self-publishing and the minimum income is reduced. Membership-at-large is open to literary agents, attorneys and accountants who represent authors, and heirs, trustees, and executors of deceased authors who would qualify for General membership. Dues are $90/year.
http://www.authorsguild.org

12) MWW (Midwest Writers Workshop) – This regional organization focuses on writing craft and networking. It offers intensive writing craft courses, agent and editor pitch sessions, and critiques at its annual conference on the campus of Ball State University in Muncie, Indiana. No membership is required. See MWW's website to sign up for the newsletter.
http://www.midwestwriters.org

Writing is often a solitary career, and joining a writing organization can provide interaction, education, and networking opportunities. If finances prohibit joining one of these groups, the local library or university may be able to provide information on private writing groups in the area. Online groups through Yahoo, Google+, and Facebook are another option, and many publishers have forums for their authors to communicate with each other. Take advantage of these options to support and be supported in the writing community!

Conferences

Ideally, as a writer's career develops, her skills improve and her knowledge about writing and publishing grows. Attending Conferences offers a hands-on approach to learning, with information on a wide variety of topics, and the opportunity to network with publisher industry professionals, editors, agents, and other authors.

Many conferences are sponsored by writing organizations and have presentations/workshops covering topics considered most beneficial to its members. The more diverse the membership, the more diverse the workshops. For example: RWA's membership includes all levels of writers, from beginners to multi-published bestselling romance authors. Their national conference reflects that diversity, with tracks on writing craft, self-publishing, research, publishing industry, career, etc.—topics designed to meet the needs of all attendees. Organizations who cater to only published authors focus on areas of interest to their members, such as the publishing industry and networking. To find out which organizations hold conferences, see the previous section on Writing Organizations for links to their websites.

Local or regional chapters may host smaller scale conferences. Some are one-day events with a single theme and one or more speakers. Others last two or three days and offer multiple topics and speakers. Agent and editor pitches are common at longer full-weekend conferences, and some have award ceremonies for their chapter contests as part of their festivities.

Cost can be a major factor in deciding which conferences to attend. National conference registration fees are typically at least double, and usually triple or quadruple, the cost of regional or local chapter conference fees. A conference with many workshops, speakers, and events will demand a higher fee. Add in the cost of hotel, meals, travel, baggage fees, parking (airport or hotel), and any extras to formulate a budget. Plan on book costs and shipping expense when a signing is part of the event. Sharing a room and travel expenses with a friend (whether driving to the conference or hiring a car service for hotel/airport transportation) are effective ways to cut costs. Check out local restaurants' online menus prior to the trip for pricing and food options if meals aren't part of the registration fee. Save receipts and record these expenses for tax purposes!

While wardrobe purchases aren't tax-deductible, they can put a dent in the budget. A conference is a professional function and authors should dress with that in mind. Business professional to business casual makes the best impression. Plan on lots of walking and standing, so comfortable shoes are a must. Dress up a casual outfit with a scarf or jewelry. Awards ceremonies are often dress-up occasions, but that doesn't necessarily mean buying a full-length gown. Do a little research to find out what appropriate dress is for the event. A simple little black dress may work well, without breaking the bank. Also, plan to be "on" at all times. Industry professionals will be in the restaurants and bars and at parties and other functions in the hotel. Sweats and ratty jeans are not a good choice if you're in the conference area.

Safety is the usually most overlooked aspect of attending conferences. Although the event hotel may seem filled with only attendees, other non-conference guests could be staying there as well. Avoid announcing room numbers in crowded areas. Discard the key card envelope in the room in case keys are lost. Use the safety latch when in the room to prevent hotel employees or other hotel guests from entering the room without knocking. Locate the nearest emergency exit. Remove nametags when leaving the conference hotel. Use the designated driver rule to ensure everyone in the group arrives back at the hotel or their rooms safely. Only accept drinks from the bartender and never leave drinks unattended. Most of all, use common sense.

Conferences are a great way for authors to improve their writing skills, learn about the publishing industry, and network with others in their field. They can also be overwhelming for a first-timer, so take a deep breath, allow for some downtime, and focus on achieving a well-rounded career!

Workshops and Online Classes

Conferences don't always fit into an author's lifestyle, schedule, or budget, but Workshops & Online Classes are available from many reliable sources for continued learning and growth. Like conference workshops and presentations, online workshops and classes cover almost every topic related to writing, publishing, and research. However, not all are of the same quality and not all instructors have the proper experience and/or knowledge to teach them. Lots of true experts offer workshops and classes, so be selective.

Many genre-specific writing organizations and RWA chapters offer great classes on topics like period costuming, crime scene investigation, and mythology—the research end of writing. Authors have a wide variety of "day jobs" or experiences that are excellent real-life resources. Check out the instructor's credentials, if possible. An emergency room doctor or nurse is a much better source of medical information than someone who watches every episode of Grey's Anatomy.

College degrees are fine, but a combination of book knowledge and applied knowledge usually provides a more accurate basis for information, especially in writing craft and publishing-related workshops and classes. A creative writing degree is much more effective when combined with actual publishing (writing and/or editing) credentials.

Authors are expected to use social media to promote themselves and their books. For the technologically challenged, the learning curve can be a steep one. Invest in online classes about using social media, creating blogs and websites, and self-promotion, taught by those familiar with marketing and the publishing industry to avoid learning pushy promotion techniques. Using social media incorrectly can be worse than not using it at all.

A few suggestions:

Kristen Lamb – Classes on writing craft, social media, and other writing/publishing-related topics. She also posts regularly about writing/publishing/marketing topics on her Warrior Writers blog. Great info!

RWA –For RWA members only. RWA University offers one or two online workshops per month. Many are free. Others are low cost ($10). Topics vary and have included Taxes for Writers, Self-Editing, and Pitch Perfect.

Genre-specific RWA chapters – Kiss of Death, FF&P, Celtic Hearts, Hearts Through History, and others offer many research-related topics. Some classes and workshops are available to non-members.

Online workshops and classes are available on almost every topic a writer might need—research, grammar/writing craft, social media, writing programs like Scrivener and OneNote, book cover design, etc. They're an affordable alternative to conferences and some conference speakers also offer the same classes in an online setting. Continued growth as an author is vital!

Conventions

Conferences, workshops, and online classes emphasize the educational aspects of writing, although some conferences offer book-signing opportunities. Conventions, on the other hand, focus on reader-author relations. Book signings are an important part of conventions, along with meet-and-greet events and a party-type atmosphere. Cover models often attend conventions, giving both authors and readers a chance to meet their favorite heroes.

The (Romantic Times) RT Booklovers Convention is one of the biggest and most popular annual conventions. Like national conferences, the registration fee can be a major expense (and is tax-deductible). RT moves from region to region each year. Most recently, the convention has been held in Chicago (2012), Kansas City (2013), and New Orleans (2014). The 2015 venue is Dallas. RT also offers workshops to attendees on a smaller scale than the typical national writers conference.
https://www.rtconvention.com/

Another popular convention is Lori Foster's Reader-Author Get Together near Cincinnati, Ohio. This event focuses on connecting romance readers and writers, offering two book signings and a variety of social gatherings for reader-author interaction. The reasonable fee is based on author or reader registration, and space is limited—currently 100 authors. RAGT is a more intimate convention due to its smaller size.
http://lorifoster.com/connect-with-lori-online/readerauthor-get-together/

Romance Novel Convention is a newer event, founded by well-known cover model Jimmy Thomas. This convention is held in Las Vegas and offers workshops, classes, and plenty of opportunities to socialize with models Jimmy works with in his successful cover art business. Registration is mid-range priced and may be discounted with all-inclusive packages.
http://romancenovelconvention.com/

RomCon consists of an educational portion for authors and a social portion for reader and author interaction. Mid-priced registration fees are based on attendance of one or both parts. RomCon offers book signings, chats, and other events for readers to talk to their favorite romance authors and meet new ones by sub-genre. The convention is held in Colorado. Author spaces are limited.
http://www.romcon.com/index.html

Authors After Dark Convention focuses on romance readers and is a mid-priced event. It offers reader-author interaction and a public book signing as well as a costume ball for paid attendees. This convention changes venues from year to year. Author spaces are limited.
http://www.authorsafterdark.org/index.html

Indie Romance Convention (IRC) offers a book signing, games, parties, and discussions for readers to interact with authors. IRC's location changes from year to year to allow readers from different regions to attend. This is another mid-priced event. Author spaces are limited.
http://indieromancecon.com/registration/

A Google search will yield more regional and genre-specific conventions. Remember that conventions are for connecting with fans and finding new ones as well as meeting other authors. The atmosphere is much more casual than a conference and gives authors a chance to directly introduce potential readers to their books.

Promotional item (swag) giveaways are a great way to attract those new readers at conventions. Some popular choices are bookmarks, trading cards, postcards, pens, fans, magnets, and jewelry. Vistaprint, Etsy shops, and many other online stores offer a wide selection of personalized items at varying prices. And that swag is tax-deductible too!

Writer's Block

What happens when an author's creativity slows to a tickle or stops altogether? Besides PANIC, Writer's Block is the most common term for the condition. What are the causes? What's the cure?

Lots of issues can lead to writer's block, but one of the most frequent causes is burnout. Authors tend to write every day, usually eight or more hours a day and close to three hundred sixty-five days a year. A few days away can recharge the brain and allow the mind to focus on something else. Writing inspiration often comes from observing—people, nature, etc. Think of the time spent on "vacation" as research.

Stress is another major factor in abandonment by the muse. Unfortunately, it's often a fact of life—but exercise can combat the effects of stress, leading to a relaxed mind and free-flowing thoughts. Diet, which may be affected by stress, can also affect mood and health, which in turn can cause stress. Break the cycle. Physical wellbeing can improve the state of the mind. Since writers tend to lead sedentary lives, proper diet and exercise can make a substantial difference in reducing writer's block as well improving stress levels and general health.

Lack of sleep and some medications can also affect the ability to focus on a story. Note taking and in-depth plotting can be helpful aids in dealing with medication-related concentration problems. Better sleep habits or daily naps may make a difference with sleep deprivation and/or insomnia-related writing issues.

Possibly the most frustrating of all causes is the story itself. Oftentimes, the author's subconscious mind notices problems with the story before the author does. Logic lapses, plot issues, and inconsistent characters aren't always immediately apparent. Does the story start in the right place? Is each scene written in the most effective POV? Setting aside the manuscript for several days reduces familiarity, and mistakes are more easily spotted on a read-through. A critique partner or beta reader can also help in these instances. Fix the issues, and the story will likely begin flowing again.

Lack of confidence is another creativity killer. Some writers need to complete multiple drafts of a single manuscript before it's ready for editing. Others edit as they go. No matter the process, writing should be as enjoyable as it is hard. Perfection isn't the immediate goal. A finished manuscript comes first. Edits and feedback follow to improve the story and/or the craft.

Take a deep breath, give the muse a boot in the behind, and WRITE!

Fear of Failure...and Success

Fear of Failure...and Success goes hand in hand with writer's block. Writers tend to be artistically minded, and lack of—or overblown—confidence often comes with the territory. Not only can self-doubt be a problem, concern over becoming successful may contribute to a stalled career. Overconfidence has its own issues and can be just as detrimental, but that's another story for another day...

Finishing a manuscript is one of the hardest feats of being a writer. Throughout that arduous journey, many authors vacillate between loving and hating their stories/writing. Is the plot good enough? Am I showing instead of telling? Are the characters likeable? Do I suck??? Critique partners and/or beta readers provide valuable feedback, but having honest and thorough yet constructive comments is vital. The worst part? No matter how well written, not everyone will like every book. Focus on education in weak areas of writing to gain confidence. Push through the low spots and try not to edit during those times.

After the editing and polishing process, submission is the next step. Will the editor/my editor/an agent/my agent like the story? What if it's rejected? Was the first book sale a fluke? The majority of published authors still suffer from a case of butterflies from hitting the send button. Rather than worrying about that submission, begin work on the next book. Practice is a far better way to improve writing craft than procrastinating for days, weeks, or months while waiting for a response. Nervousness is normal, but agonizing over a submission can be crippling. Writers write as an escape. Use it to your advantage!

The manuscript has sold or gotten a thumbs-up from the editor/agent/freelance editor/critique partners. Now, authors get to fixate on whether or not the book will sell to readers. Will it get good reviews? Will it make a bestsellers list? Will I make enough money to quit the day job? Do I need to market more? What kind of marketing should I be doing?

Again, rather than focusing on all those questions and possible scenarios, writers need to work on the next book. Yes, this is a never-ending cycle. This is what makes writing a career.

It sounds difficult, doesn't it? It is.

Fear of success can also cause an author to subconsciously derail her career before it starts.

But...what if my book sells 10,000 copies the first week? Can I write another book that's just as good? Will I be a one-hit wonder? I have to interact with readers? I don't know how to do that! Interviews??? I'm an introvert! I can't go out and meet people! Public appearances? Every day is a bad hair day!

Take a few deep breaths. Put that active imagination to work on a book. Write for the joy of writing.

On to the most important questions...
Why am I writing? Am I writing to satisfy an inner need or simply to make money? Do I need to write to make myself happy?

The answers help define the fear. Someone who's in it only for the money doesn't usually put her heart and soul into every story. She doesn't have as much to lose by submitting, publishing, and waiting for sales numbers. Produce, produce, produce is the object of the game for her.

However, the love of writing doesn't have to mean suffering through the "Am I good enough?" complex. Keep things in perspective. A great book may not produce great sales and great reviews. Bestseller doesn't necessarily equate best-written story. That's reality, not a judgment of any person's ability to write. Telling a heartfelt story is the top priority. Authors should please themselves first and spend less time consumed by the need for approval and acceptance. Make your own confidence.

Repeat after me. "I am a writer. I'll learn what I need to learn to become a better writer."

Did you notice the lack of adjectives in the first sentence? Awful, good, great... What do they matter? A writer IS a writer. Craft and industry knowledge can be learned, and even great writers never stop seeking that knowledge in this ever-changing publishing world.

I am a writer. I'll learn what I need to learn to become a better writer.

Goal Setting

To have a successful career in publishing, authors must sell books and produce new releases on a regular basis. In order to complete new works, many writers use Goal Setting to stay on track and meet deadlines. A combination of short- and long-term goals can help writers achieve success, on a small or large scale.

Goals can include daily/weekly/monthly/annual target word counts, self-imposed deadlines for chapters/manuscripts/series, meeting sales goals, making a bestseller list, winning a prestigious contest, etc. They can also include attending conferences, conventions, and workshops. Book signings can be part of an author's goals too.

Word counts depend on many factors. Authors may have other jobs or careers in addition to writing. Some have children or older parents to care for. By setting achievable goals, a writer can make progress while not putting too much pressure on herself. Ten thousand words a day may be doable for some, and others are able to write a chapter or a thousand words. Track progress and avoid comparison to others.

Deadlines can be effective for those who work well under pressure, but be sure to set realistic deadlines. A set-up for failure won't help the creative process. Slower writers may need to complete two or more manuscripts before submission or self-publication to ensure timely releases.

Book sales have a direct correlation to a bestseller list goal. However, a lot of marketing and promotion time goes into making those sales. Time spent on marketing and promo is time not spent writing. Word counts and deadlines may require adjustment to take those aspects into consideration. Budgeting comes into play as well.

Contest finals/wins can increase exposure and, subsequently, sales.

Entering contests can be costly and time-consuming, and each author has to weigh the benefits versus the expenses. Is it a good return on investment?

Conferences, conventions, workshops, and book signings also mean time away from writing. They all have their advantages, though. Improving writing craft and learning about the publishing industry help authors grow. Reader interaction is important for maintaining readership and increasing it. Are they good choices for a writer's career?

Use goal setting to map out a good mix of writing, promotion, and education by budgeting both time and money. Assess which activities help achieve designated goals. Adjust when necessary!

Balance

While writing is a full-time career for many authors, not all are able to sit at their computers for six or more uninterrupted hours each day. In fact, the vast majority of writers must Balance numerous demands on their time. Many have part- or full-time jobs in or out of the home. Some have young children or ill family members to care for. Those who homeschool their kids have an important responsibility to fulfill as well. Children's extracurricular activities or a job requiring travel can mean lots of time spent on the road and at various venues. Laundry, grocery shopping, meals. And a clean house—what's that???

That doesn't even take into consideration the time required for social media, promotion, attending events, etc. in relation to having a writing career. The list goes on and on. What about writing time???

Finding a way to balance it all can add stress to an already hectic life. Unfortunately, no single template will work for everyone. The non-writing demands for every author differ greatly and every writer has a method that fits her situation best. Create a manageable calendar with reasonable and realistic goals. Above all, resist comparison to other authors.

Prioritize...
Make a list of those things that require a scheduled or unscheduled commitment each day or certain days.
What non-writing jobs/tasks must be done at or by a specified time?
-Day/night job
-Childcare
-Caregiver
-Homeschooler
-Transportation to and/or from school activities
-Meals
-Pay bills

Other variable responsibilities or activities:
-Laundry
-Volunteer work
-Housekeeping
-Doctor/dentist/vet appointments
-Grocery shopping
-Vacation
-Holidays/birthday parties/anniversaries
-Family time
-Exercise

What writing jobs/tasks must be done at or by a specified time?
-Book deadlines/submissions
-Events/appearances/signings
-Writing chapter meetings
-Blog appearances/scheduled posts
-Contest entry judging

Other variable responsibilities or activities:
-Recordkeeping
-Email
-Website updates
-Social media/promotion
-Critiquing/beta reading
Writing...
What time of day is the most effective for writing?
Are publisher- or self-established deadlines achievable with reasonable and realistic word count goals?
Is the location/atmosphere conducive to successful writing?
Is the plotter/pantser/plantser approach still working well?
Are current critique partners/beta readers offering constructive feedback?
Is the current manuscript the best one to write at this time?

Schedule...
Even if the times vary, penciling in tentative writing times can provide enough motivation to stay on track. A calendar also

provides a visual account of available time to help establish good writing goals and make adjustments to non-essential activities. Less wasted time means more writing time.

Relaxation time, family/friends time, and self time are also important in the balance. Authors can avoid the set-up for failure and finally achieve balance with the most basic of schedules, one that lays out exactly what must be accomplished each day or year, or anything in between.

Take a deep breath. Prioritize. Schedule. Write.

Reviews

Reviews...the coveted, the uplifting, the ego-killers. They can help produce sales and make books eligible for certain types of paid promotion and advertising. Or they can adversely affect a writer's state of mind.

Every author wants readers to love her stories—it's human nature. However, reading (bad) reviews can lead to writer's block, fear of failure, and bad behavior for the unprepared. Here are some rules to live by:

Rule #1: Not everyone will like the book. Award winning, best written, bestseller—none of it matters. Each reader will have his/her own opinion, which may or may not be the same as the author's or another reader's.

Rule #2: Grow a thick skin. Agent and editor rejections are usually polite, if impersonal at times. Reviews can be scathing and blunt.

Rule #3: Avoid reading reviews. Yes, a great review can boost the ego, but a bad one can affect writing. Writers write. Reviewers review. Keep them separate.

Rule #4: Bad reviews might actually help sales. Curiosity can lead to readers wanting to know why a book was rated low.

Rule #5: Sometimes, authors review books for the sole purpose of giving low ratings. Retaliation is tempting. Following through lowers the author to the author-reviewer's level. Rise above and maintain professionalism. Do not encourage readers to behave in the same manner as the author-reviewer, either.

Rule #6: Professional reviewers may or may not like authors thanking them for reviews. Tread carefully.

Rule #7: Screen reviewers before sending ARCs and books. Some reviewers pirate free review copies. Talk to other authors and choose wisely.

Rule #8: Ask readers to leave reviews and ratings on retail sites, Goodreads, etc. politely, without pressure, and occasionally rather than frequently. Begging is unbecoming.

Rule #9: Reviews can be personal attacks on the author and may contain inaccurate plot, character, and story references. They may also be poorly written, with bad grammar and horrendous spelling. Let the review speak for itself. Most readers will recognize an unhelpful review when they see one.

Rule #10: Do not respond to negative reviews. Repeat. Do NOT respond to negative reviews. Say it with me. DO NOT RESPOND TO NEGATIVE REVIEWS. Defending a book can quickly become a lose-lose situation. Close the browser window and step away from the keyboard. Do. Not. Respond.

Reviews are simply another part of a writing career, and maintaining a professional demeanor is vital in the publishing world. With today's instant social media network, an author's single bout of bad behavior can spread to Twitter, Facebook, Google+, etc. with a single click, resulting in lost readers and potential readers. Agents and editors will think twice about working with an author who makes a public misstep. Be the author those professional colleagues and contacts will respect.

Piracy

Piracy can be one of the most infuriating issues for writers. In this digital age, the practice of stealing artists' work is far more prevalent than pre-internet days. Although pirates have been copying music and movies and distributing those illegal copies for decades, the ability to upload files has changed the landscape. Any artwork that exists online—music, movies, photographs, books, etc.—is a target for people who participate in the criminal activity known as piracy.

Pirates and those who frequent pirate sites are, more often than not, people who wouldn't normally purchase the work they're stealing. Some simply believe art should be free. Most just want to get something for nothing, whether they really want it or not. Unfortunately, other sources of pirated books include reviewers and contest winners.
What's an author to do?

Authors can locate (some) pirated works with Google alerts and by using paid services like Muso to search for them. DMCA (Digital Millennium Copyright Act) takedown notices are sent by authors and publishers to pirate sites for the removal of pirated files. However, DMCA is US copyright law and many pirate sites are based overseas. Effectiveness of takedown notices is questionable at best for sites located outside the US since they aren't subject to the laws. In some cases, users download viruses or have personal information stolen from pirates. Payback???

Few authors and their books avoid piracy. It's a battle with no end. If the site removes the files, will they reappear a few days later? Do I want to give up writing time to deal with this side of the publishing business? Do the people who download books from pirate sites actually read them? Is it truly a lost sale?

Yes, piracy is wrong, but each author must weigh the pros and cons of conducting searches or paying for someone else to do the searching and sending takedown notices.

Go to the source. If a review site upload seems to coincide with pirated copies popping up, reconsider using that review site. Research reviewers and choose carefully. For contests, give gift codes or gift cards rather than the actual e-book file. Some contest participants and blog commenters are serial entrants with the sole purpose of uploading their winnings to file-sharing sites.

Another must—NEVER post the link to a pirate site on social media. Shaming doesn't work and the source may be inadvertently shared with the wrong people. Share with authors in private to avoid guiding more users to sources of pirated books.

A combination of prevention and takedown notices can reduce the number of pirated copies, but the reality remains that in a digital society, piracy will not disappear. Be proactive, and leave time and emotion for writing.

Hybridization

Authors have many choices in today's publishing world—traditional, small press, digital first, e-press, self-pub. The best part is being able to choose more than one, otherwise known as Hybridization.

What makes a hybrid author?

A writer who uses two or more publishing platforms for her work is said to be a hybrid author. Examples: a series contracted to an e-press, a different series self-published, another series published by a digital-first publisher, and a three-book contract with a traditional publisher OR two self-published books and a series published by an e-press with POD. Any combination of traditional, e-published, and/or self-published is defined as hybrid.

Why go hybrid?

By publishing through multiple venues, an author builds a strong foundation for her career. If one publisher goes out of business, she has other publishing options to make her work available to readers. Income stops from only one source.

Publishers can and do shut their doors. It happens quite often with small e-publishers. Some are in business to make money from authors' books by not paying royalties on time or at all. If an author chooses to write for a single publishing company, she risks losing her sole source of writing income.

The Big 6 has shrunk to the Big 5 and will likely fall to the Big 4 soon. If a traditionally published author is dropped by these less-risk-taking publishers, she needs a safety net in place. Starting over with a new publishing house is difficult for the vast majority of writers. Expanding, while having an existing career, isn't nearly as stressful.

Not all royalties are paid on the same schedule. Hybrid authors may receive payments more frequently than single-house authors—monthly, quarterly, or biannually, depending on the publisher or self-publishing venue.

More publishing platforms can mean more exposure and more readers. This is especially true of e-presses (digital only, digital first, and digital/print). Many have loyal customers because they have a large selection of genre- or sub-genre-specific books. When buyers encounter new authors on the site, they often purchase based on their experience with the publisher.

Although self-publishing currently yields higher royalty rates, those rates may decrease as supersized vendors adjust their business plans. What is now a 70% royalty on a $3.99 book may become 60% or lower without much warning.

Diversification gives authors a bit of job stability in these unpredictable days. Keep the options open and look out for that writing career. What's your backup plan?

Becoming a published author is easier than ever before with the advent of e-publishing and self-publishing. Writers have more choices for getting their books in the hands of readers and more avenues for promoting their work. They also have much more to learn about the publishing industry, social media, and marketing. As with writing craft, knowledge and ongoing education is vital. Create a writing career. Grow a writing career. Maintain a writing career.

About the Author

When her fingers aren't attached to her keyboard, **Mellanie Szereto** enjoys hiking, Pilates, cooking, gardening, and researching for her stories. Many times, the research partners with her other hobbies, taking her from the Hocking Hills region in Ohio to the Colorado Rockies or the Adirondacks of New York. Sometimes, the trip is no farther than her garden for ingredients and her kitchen to test recipes for her latest steamy tale. She is multi-published with Siren-Bookstrand and has a new self-published foodie contemporary series, *Love on the Menu*, in addition to her nonfiction book, *Writing Tip Wednesday: The Writing Craft Handbook,* based on her informational blog series. Mellanie makes her home in rural Indiana with her husband of twenty-eight years, their son, and two cats. She is a member of Romance Writers of America, Indiana Romance Writers of America, Hearts Through History Romance Writers, and PASIC.

Visit her website: http://www.mellanieszereto.com

Read her blog: http://www.mellanieszereto.blogspot.com

Like her on Facebook:
http://www.facebook.com/authormellanieszereto

Follow her on Twitter: http://www.twitter.com/mellanieszereto

Find her on Goodreads:
http://www.goodreads.com/mellanie_szereto

If you enjoyed this book, please consider rating or leaving a review on the retailer's website and/or Goodreads. Thanks!

Other books by Mellanie Szereto

Writing Tip Wednesday Handbooks
    Writing Tip Wednesday: The Writing Craft Handbook

Love on the Menu series
    Love Served Hot

The Sextet Anthologies
    Volume 1: Sharing
    Volume 2: Dirty Dancing
    Volume 3: Occupational Hazards
    Volume 4: Entanglements
    Volume 5: Mistletoe & Ménage

The Sextet Presents…
    Playing in the Raine: A Toy Story
    Bound by Voodoo: Legends

Bewitching Desires series
    Two if by Sea
    Two Knights of Passion
    Two Fated for One
    Two Pirates to Treasure
    Two Times the Trouble
    Two Roped and Ready
    Two from the Triangle
    Beyond Bewitched

Notes